Confidence:
The Missing Substance
of Faith

by
Creflo A. Dollar Jr.

If you would like more information about this ministry, or are interested in becoming a partner, please write:
WORLD CHANGERS MINISTRIES
Post Office Box 490124
College Park, Georgia 30349

Editorial and Creative services provided by:
Vision Communications
169 E. 32nd
Edmond, OK 73013
(405) 348-7995

Cover design by:
Virgil Lynn Design
405-348-7965

Unless otherwise indicated, all Scripture quotations are from the KING JAMES VERSION.

NIV – New International Version
AMP – Amplified Version

Confidence: The Missing Substance of Faith
ISBN: 0-9634781-3-3

Table of Contents

Confidence: The Missing Substance of Faith

Chapter 1
The Missing Ingredient

"The Lord shall be thy confidence, and shall keep thy foot from being taken." Proverbs 3:26

Do you see results every time you pray? Does your faith always produce that for which you're believing and confessing? Are you seeing the full manifestation of God's promises of healing, provision and deliverance in your daily life?

If you're like most believers, the answer to those questions is a frustrated "no." For many Christians, prayer is more like a roll of the dice than an exercise in faith.

Instead of "Oooooh, give me a seven...," it's "Ooooooh, Lord! Let it work, Jesus! Please God, do something about my situation!"

Other times we resort to "bargaining" with God in an attempt to get Him to move on our behalf. "I'll love you forever, Lord. I'll tithe 15%!.....20%!....just help me, Lord!"

Perhaps you've even resorted to a "fleece" in an attempt to gain some assurance that God was going to meet your needs. "Lord, if you're really in this, have someone come up to me today and say the word 'igloo.' Then I'll really know it's you."

You probably recognized yourself in one or more of the above examples. I think we've all been there at one time or another in our Christian lives. I don't need to tell you, all that straining and striving to get God to move on your behalf can be a baffling and disheartening experience. Well, I've got news for you. Not only does that kind of prayer not work very well, it's totally unnecessary!

God never intended His children to beg, plead and bargain for His promises to be fulfilled in their lives. His earnest desire is that you experience the full manifesta-

1

tion of every promise in His Word. That means total provision, prosperity, absolute health, well-being and deliverance from all oppression.

Then why aren't most Christians, in spite of all their confessing, believing and "claiming," experiencing that kind of life? Why are we still bombarding heaven with "roll the dice" prayers and "let's make a deal" petitions? The answer is profoundly simple.

Each of the methods of praying mentioned above has a common missing element. They lack the one key component that will energize your faith and revolutionize your prayer life. That missing ingredient is <u>confidence</u>.

What is Confidence?

Once you start looking for it, you'll be amazed how often the word confidence appears in scripture.

When the Bible uses the word confidence it means "assurance" or complete and total "persuasion." It also closely parallels the meaning of "trust." When you trust something, you have confidence in it.

When it rains, I open my umbrella, *confident* that it will keep the rain off. I *trust* it to keep me dry.

Confidence is the quality which leads you to stand up under or endure adversity. It causes you to undertake a difficult task with diligence. You'll never take a firm standing for something without confidence.

Another term closely identified with confidence is "boldness." In fact, boldness can often be used interchangeably with confidence when talking about spiritual principles. That's because, in scripture, both words are derived from the very same Greek root word.

Don't get the wrong idea, though. A lot of us have a distorted concept of what boldness is. Many people think boldness is seeing how loud you can talk and how belligerent you can be. That's not boldness. That's flesh.

Finally, boldness is intricately tied up with the concepts of "yieldedness" and "obedience."

Their can be no true obedience where there is no confidence. Nor can you yield yourself to someone whom you don't trust.

Is confidence the final piece of the faith puzzle for you? Read on and find out.

Chapter 2
The Power of Confidence

I've heard it dozens of times. "Pastor Dollar, I know I have faith, yet my faith doesn't seem to be producing anything."

If you can identify with that complaint, I've got good news for you. There's probably nothing wrong with your faith. You may simply be lacking the vital ingredient of confidence.

Confidence is the force that launches your faith. It propels faith forward like the rocket boosters send the Space Shuttle into orbit. Trying to operate your faith without the force of confidence is like trying to take off in an airplane that has no engines. There's probably nothing wrong with the structure of the plane. It's simply missing a crucial element.

"But, Pastor Dollar! I've confessed prosperity scriptures over and over and my bills still aren't getting paid." Child of God, you can quote scripture until you're hoarse, but if confidence doesn't rise up and propel your faith, it will never reach its destination.

Saying words is not enough. Even acting on those words is not enough. You must have confidence in those words for them to have the power to change your circumstances.

Think of it this way. Have you ever seen a mother take her small child to the bus stop and put him on the school bus? Confidence is the mother that takes faith by the hand, leads it to the bus stop, and sends it on its way to its destination. It is the force that energizes and activates your words.

Just because you say something doesn't mean those words are full of confidence. The difference is often apparent. It's like a singer who stands up on a stage and with a weak trembling voice, squeaks out a song. Then someone else gets up and sings the very same song, belting it out with enthusiasm. One singer sings with confidence, the other just sings.

Fill Up Your Words

Don't misunderstand. Words are important. But words alone cannot change your circumstances. Simply think of them as spiritual containers. Faith is poured into your words by the force of confidence.

Imagine an empty glass beside a pitcher of water. In order for the glass to become full of water, some force has to move the pitcher and pour the water into it.

Confidence is that force which pours the water in the pitcher (faith that comes by hearing the Word of God) into the glass (your words). Simply put, confidence pours faith into your words and the faith-filled words go into action!

The missing link in many believer's faith life is confidence. We've had the faith. We've had the corresponding action that must accompany faith. What we've lacked is the force of confidence to get the whole process moving.

We've wanted the water in the glass but we've not been able to get it from the pitcher into the glass because we haven't understood the importance of confidence.

It's Not Over 'Til It's Over

What does confidence look like? A good example can be found in Habakkuk 3:17,18:

Although the fig tree shall not blossom, neither shall fruit be in the vines; the labour of the olive shall fail, and the fields shall yield no meat; the flock shall be cut off from the fold, and there shall be no herd in the stalls: Yet I will rejoice in the LORD, I will joy in the God of my salvation.

Now here's a man with confidence. His crops have failed. His livestock is destroyed. Nothing is going right.

5

But what is his response to these dire circumstances? "Yet..." He says "Yet I will rejoice in the Lord..."

Why is he so optimistic in the face of incredible adversity? Read on:

The LORD God is my strength, and he will make my feet like hinds feet, and he will make me to walk upon mine high places. v.18

Child of God, it's not over until it's over. And it's not over until you either win or quit. Like Habakkuk, you've got to make sure your confidence isn't dependent upon your surrounding circumstances.

You must know—even though the light bill is due, the gas bill is due, the phone company is threatening to disconnect you and your paycheck just bounced—the Lord, somehow, someway is going to bring you through. You've got to make the Lord your confidence.

Chapter 3
Understanding the Force
of Confidence

When you're full of confidence, you know that you know that you know that God's Word is going to produce exactly what it says it will. And that's not only when the circumstances look good. True confidence is fully persuaded no matter *what* the circumstances look like.

How do you develop that kind of confidence? We'll look at that in detail later. Before you can begin to cultivate the kind of confidence that will move your faith into the stratosphere, you must first have a greater biblical understanding of what it is and how it works.

Fully Persuaded
And [Abraham] being fully persuaded that, what he had promised, he was able to perform.
Romans 4:21

As I said at the outset, you can define confidence as the state of being "fully persuaded." The above verse points to Abraham as a person of great confidence.

You'll remember that Abraham was 100 years old and his wife Sarah was 90 when the Lord told them, "I'm going to bless you with a boy and your descendants are going to outnumber the stars."

Of course, Abraham and Sarah didn't reach the point of being fully persuaded right away. In fact, when God's promise seemed a little slow in coming they decided to help God out.

Sarah arranged for her personal servant, Hagar, to be with Abraham. The result was a son—Ishmael. But that was not what God had promised. The previously barren Sarah was the one who, along with Abraham, would bear a child whose seed would bless all nations of the earth.

That couldn't happen, however, until Abraham got to the point of being fully persuaded, or in other words, the place of confidence.

Child of God, this is where most of us miss it. We never become fully persuaded that God will do what He has promised in His Word.

We read a promise in scripture, then timidly tiptoe into a confession or action that is supposed to resemble faith. The problem is that everything we say and do lacks confidence.

It's like hiring an employee to do a job that he is reluctant to do. It shows up in the quality of his work. He may go through the motions but it's obvious his heart isn't in it.

Ultimately, Abraham became absolutely, totally convinced that God was faithful to keep His promises. He reached the point of being fully persuaded. Another way of saying it is "blessed assurance."

When you receive blessed assurance, you get an empowerment that only comes from God. It's a supernatural conviction that what God has promised will indeed come to pass.

It was only when Abraham reached that point that the promise of God could be manifested in the natural realm. The same is true for you. You'll never see the miraculous manifestations of God's promises in your life until you reach the point of being fully persuaded.

Hold On Tight!

Once you've developed confidence in a promise of God, the next thing you must do is hold on to it.

But Christ as a son over his own house; whose house are we, if we hold fast the confidence and the rejoicing of the hope firm unto the end. For we are made partakers of Christ, if we hold the beginning of our confidence stedfast unto the end; Hebrews 3:6,14

If you want to receive the promises of God in your life, you must hold tightly to your confidence until the end. When is the end? When you have the manifestation of the promise in which you place your confidence.

Never let go of your confidence until you've received your miracle. In other words, "It's not over until it's over."

Don't think for a minute that holding on is going to be easy, however. If you're standing on a promise from God's Word, the devil is going to pull out every trick in his bag to try to get you to let go of your confidence.

He'll use well-meaning family members, friends, television and any other voice at his disposal to try to shake your faith in God's promise.

If you're believing God for healing, hold fast until your healing manifests. If you're trusting God's Word concerning finances, hang on with a grip of steel until your situation turns around. No matter how long it takes, hold on.

Notice verse 14 again. "...if we hold the beginning of our confidence stedfast until the end;"

That tells us confidence has a beginning and an end. Often the beginning of confidence comes when we sow seeds. If you need money, sow financial seeds. Sow them into good soil and above all, sow them in confidence.

If you need health, sow seeds of healing by praying for the sick. And whatever you do, sow those seeds in confidence that they will produce a hundredfold. That is how confidence has its beginning.

A confident beginning is not "hoping and praying." You can't sow seeds "hoping" that you will see a return. There is no confidence in that.

If God said it, He will do it. He cannot lie. He framed the entire universe with the power and integrity of His Word. If He told one lie, all in existence would disintegrate.

Confidence. Begin every journey of faith with it and hold on to it until the end.

Claim Your Reward

Satan is determined to get you to turn loose of your confidence. Why? Because he hates you and doesn't want you to receive your reward. That's right! Confidence always produces a reward.

Cast not away therefore your confidence, which hath <u>great recompence of reward</u>. Hebrews 10:35

Don't cast away (throw away, toss aside, let go of) your confidence. It's just what the devil wants you to do. In fact, he knows that if he can destroy your confidence in God's faithfulness and in His Word, you're finished.

Be on guard. The enemy probably won't come in and try to wipe out your confidence all at one time. Instead, he'll try to erode it away, a little bit at a time.

A little word of discouragement spoken here. A little bad news there. Before long, if you're not watchful, you'll find your confidence collapsing around you like a house of cards.

Don't cast away your confidence. Hang on and claim your reward.

Confidence is your Foundation

For the Lord shall be thy confidence, and shall keep thy foot from being taken. Proverbs 3:26

Having the Lord as your confidence will keep your foot from stumbling. What is the foot used for? Standing. It supports your stance. In Ephesians 6:13,14 we're told "..having done all to stand. Stand...."

When you're standing immovable upon God's Word you're in a position to receive great blessing. The devil will try to move you from that stand. But when you make the Lord your confidence, you can be assured that your foot will remain firm.

Confidence is Your Strength
For thus saith the Lord GOD, the Holy One of Israel; In returning and rest shall ye be saved; in quietness and in confidence shall be your strength: Isaiah 30:15

When you're fighting the good fight of faith, it is crucial that you have sufficient strength for the battle. Spiritual strength can mean the difference between prosperity and poverty, deliverance and oppression, sickness and health, even life and death.

How do you gain spiritual strength? According to this verse, through confidence!

The strength that comes through confidence will get you into the Word when you think you're too tired to study. It will get you up for a time of fellowship with God when your flesh would rather stay in bed. It will get you to church to be fed the Word when your body is demanding to be plopped onto the couch. Confidence is the strength of your faith.

Praying With Confidence
This is the <u>confidence</u> we have in approaching God: that if we ask anything according to his will, he hears us. And if we know that he hears us— whatever we ask—we know that we have what we asked of him. I John 5:14,15 (NIV)

Prayer doesn't accomplish much until it's energized by the force of confidence.

There is nothing quite as powerful as a prayer that you know in your knower is going to come to pass. How does that kind of faith come about?

First, through confidence that God hears you when you pray. That's where you start. "I know that when I pray, God hears me."

Then you have to be confident that you're praying in accordance with the will of God. How do you do that? By praying the Word. God's Word is His will.

Find a promise in God's Word that speaks to your particular situation. Then pray it and stand on it. "I know that I'm praying God's will because I'm praying His Word."

Following those two steps, comes the confidence that you have that for which you pray. When you pray with confidence, things happen.

Chapter 4
Developing Confidence

So far, we've seen that confidence is the missing link in the chain of faith—the force that launches your faith into motion. It's the trigger that enables your faith to work the same way every time.

That's important because God wants you to know exactly how to get your healing, your bills paid, or whatever it is you need and get them every time.

Once you understand the role of confidence, there is no reason to continue to live your Christian life in frustration and defeat.

"I'm convinced Brother Dollar! I want confidence. But how do I get it?" That's a fair question and we'll find the answer in the Word of God.

Let's look at some scriptural conditions and steps to developing the force of confidence.

A Heart That Is True
Let us draw near with <u>a true heart in full assurance of faith</u>, having our hearts sprinkled from an evil conscience, and our bodies washed with pure water. Let us hold fast the profession of our faith without wavering; (for he is faithful that promised;)Hebrews 10:22,23

If you want to deal with God and His Word with full assurance (another term for confidence), you must first have a "true heart."

Don't go to God with a bunch of lies and manipulation. Go to Him with a true heart. If you've made mistakes, if you've sinned, admit it. God wants the truth no matter how ugly it is.

When you come to God and say "Lord, I have sinned today," you're operating with a true heart. That level of honesty and transparency is a beautiful thing to God. The

13

result? You are able to draw near to him with confidence—"in full assurance of faith."

What is the full assurance of faith? Confident faith. Don't come to God with faith alone. Come with confidence too. Confidence in God's goodness. Confidence in the Word. Confidence in God's mercy and grace to cleanse you from all unrighteousness. Confidence in your position in Christ Jesus. Confidence in the faith life.

A true heart is a prerequisite to that kind of confidence.

In whatever our hearts in [tormenting] self-accusation make us feel guilty and condemn us. For [we are in God's hands]; He is above and greater than our consciences (our hearts), and He knows (perceives and understands) everything—nothing is hidden from Him.

And, beloved, if our consciences (our hearts) do not accuse us—if they do not make us feel guilty and condemn us—we have CONFIDENCE (complete assurance and boldness) before God, And we receive from Him whatever we ask,...
I John 3:20-22a (AMP)

What other people know about you is not as important as what you and God know about yourself. When you know that there is sin in your life and your heart is accusing you and making you feel guilty and condemned, it becomes very difficult to have confidence in God answering your prayer.

Keeping your heart intact is extremely important if you are to have confidence towards God.

"...We have Confidence before God, And we receive from Him whatever we ask,..."

Conceive Your Miracle

Are you beginning to grasp the relationship between confidence and faith? Do you see why it's pointless to confess "by His stripes I am healed." when you have no confidence in those words? Your words are only empty containers. It takes both confidence and faith to produce results in your life.

One day as I was meditating on the correlation between faith and confidence, the Spirit of God spoke to me and said, "They are mating." This surprised me at first but the more I thought about it the more I understood the truth of what He was saying.

A woman can't have a baby alone. Nor can a man have one without a woman. It takes both to create offspring.

The same is true with faith and confidence. When they come together, the thing that you are believing God for is conceived. Hold on to that confidence long enough and it will be birthed. At that point you'll see the physical manifestation of that which was conceived in the spirit— your miracle.

The Tradition Trap

As we have seen, the Word of God is a powerful thing. Yet there is something that can stop it from operating effectively for you—tradition. Specifically, religious tradition.

Jesus once told a religious crowd that their traditions had rendered the Word of God of no effect (Mark 7:13). Many believers have been taught through the religious traditions of various denominations that God doesn't work wonders any more. "The age of miracles has passed," we're told. As a result they have no confidence in God's promises of miraculous deliverance, healing and provision.

Many others have come up in Pentecostal or charismatic churches. They've seen manifestations of this or that. They've seen great men of power and anointing minister. Yet they have no confidence that what they've seen can ever be a part of their own lives. They simply go through the motions without ever seeing any real results.

15

This reinforces their lack of confidence. It's a downward cycle of despair and frustration.

But praise God, the cycle works the other way too! One day you hear the Word of God and really begin to understand it. Confidence and faith begin to rise up in your spirit. You step out and believe God for a little miracle. Perhaps you need some food. And by faith you receive a hamburger.

Then later, when you need a bill paid and there's no money left, you remember how the Word worked when you needed a meal. More faith and confidence rise up within you. Together they go to work and your need is miraculously met. It's an upward cycle of ever-increasing faith, confidence and power.

Expect Opposition

Operating in confidence does not mean that you will not encounter adversity.

But even after that we had suffered before, and were shamefully entreated, as ye know, at Philippi, we were bold in our God to speak unto you the gospel of God with much contention.
I Thessalonians 2:2

If you plan to reap the rewards of walking in confidence and boldness (remember: the two are synonymous), you'd better get ready for some contention.

Just as with Paul, controversy, contention and opposition tend to follow a person of true boldness. Therefore, it's vital that you learn how to hold on to your confidence in the midst of such resistance.

The three Hebrew boys Nebuchadnezzar threw into the fiery furnace are a great example of confidence under pressure. Their response to his death threat was:

If it be so, our God whom we serve is able to deliver us from the burning fiery furnace, and he will deliver us out of thine hand, O king. Daniel 3:17

Can you hear their confidence? "We don't care what you do to us. We are not going to bow down and worship your idols. We are fully persuaded that our God is able to deliver us!"

Daniel is another great example. His boldness in prayer caused contention. As a result he ended up in a dungeon full of hungry lions.

If most of us found ourselves in those circumstances we'd be lunch! But Daniel's quiet confidence put his faith in motion. Faith brought angels on the scene to shut the watering mouths of those lions.

Why does contention always follow bold believers. Because it is designed by Satan to destroy their confidence. He knows that if he can take away your calm assurance through trouble, strife and opposition, then your faith will lose the jets that put it into flight.

Hold on to your confidence in the face of contention. If you do, you will come out on top just as surely as Paul, Daniel and those three Hebrew boys did.

Chapter 5
You Can Walk in Confidence

Confidence, the kind of boldness that puts your faith into motion, is really not a complicated thing to develop. You don't need a lot of degrees or education. You don't have to be extremely intelligent, sophisticated or refined.

No matter who you are, you can have mountain moving confidence. How? You can get it the same way a couple of simple fishermen from Galilee did:

Now when they saw the boldness of Peter and John, and perceived that they were unlearned and ignorant men, they marvelled; and they took knowledge of them, that they had been with Jesus. Acts 4:13

Peter and John had boldness you could not only hear but see! How do you get confidence like that? Spend time with Jesus. Spend time with Him in prayer. Fellowship with Him in worship. Get to know Him in His Word.

Show me a person that is fully persuaded and I'll show you a person that has been with Jesus.

Ask and You Shall Receive

Ultimately, the most powerful key to developing confidence is the most simple one of all. Ask for it.

And now, Lord, behold their threatenings: and grant unto thy servants, that with all boldness they may speak thy word,... And when they [the disciples] had prayed, the place was shaken where they were assembled together; and they were all filled with the Holy Ghost, and they spake the word of God with boldness. Acts 4:29, 31

When New Testament church was faced with opposition and threats, they came together and prayed for boldness. They prayed and they were filled. It's as simple as that.

Child of God, nothing produces confidence in you like being filled with the Holy Ghost. And the Holy Ghost is yours for the asking.

If ye then, being evil, know how to give good gifts unto your children: how much more shall your heavenly Father give the Holy Spirit to them that ask him? Luke 11:13

You don't ever have to be without the force of confidence again. Imagine never again praying without knowing that your prayer was heard and answered. Never again laying hands on someone without knowing that power would flow out of you to touch that person's body. Never tithing or giving without knowing that you were going to receive back a hundredfold return.

All that and much more is possible when you unleash the force of confidence and join it to your faith.

Tape Series by Pastor Creflo A. Dollar Jr.

The Acts of the Apostle
Adjusting the Mind for Victory
The Believer's Position in Grace
The Blood Covenant: The Covenant of Strong
    Friendship
The Body of Christ
The Book of Ephesians
The Book of Hebrews
The Book of Revelation (Chapters 1–11)
The Book of Revelation (Chapters 12–22)
The Book of Romans (Chapters 1–8)
The Book of Romans (Chapters 8–14)
The Call to Sanctification
Cutting the Keys for Victory — 1992 Church
    Anniversary
Day of Discovery
The Development of the Spirit, Soul and Body
Excellence in Ministry
Excelling into the Excellence of God
Faithfulness
The Fear of God
The Foundation of Unshakable Faith
Forces of the Reborn Spirit
Getting Real about the Things of God
God's Plan for Maturity through Divine Order
Going through the Furnace
The Gospel According to Saint Mark (Chapters 1–8)
The Gospel According to Saint Mark (Chapters 9–16)
Guidance
Holiness: The Way of Life
The Holy Spirit
How to Obtain Strong Faith
The Importance of Being an Overcomer
The Intermingling of Faith and Meditation
Jesus Christ the Example
The Joy of the Lord

Tape Series by Pastor Creflo A. Dollar Jr.

The Blessings of Obedience

The Blood Covenant

By Faith in His Presence

Confidence: The Missing Substance of Faith

The Creative Power of Words

Deliverance from Lasciviousness

Destroying the Root of Debt

The Divine Order of Faith:
From the Problem to the Answer

Enemies of Faith

Faith, Foolishness or Presumption

Family and Marriage Convention '92

Forces of the Reborn Spirit

Foundation Principles of the Christian Life

Freedom from Fear

The Fruit of the Spirit

God Wants You Healed – Healing Convention 1992

God's Blessing of Prosperity

God's Plan for the Christian Family

God's Purpose for the Anointing

The Grand Finale – The Book of Revelation

Hearing and Obeying God's Voice

Hindrances to Faith

How to...By God's Word

How to Defeat the Devil

How to Experience a Deeper Life in Prayer

Intercessory Prayer

The Law of Harvest
Lifestyle of Faith
Man's Heart: The Workshop of God
The Mercies of God
Obtaining the Wealth of the Wicked
Overcoming Faith
The Power of the Anointed Word
The Power and Integrity of God's Word
Prayer: The Rock of Success
The Price to Pay to Hear from God
Pride or Humility: You Choose
The Principles of Praise
The Rejuvenation of Faith
The Rejuvenation of Prayer
The Seven Steps of Answered Prayers
Spiritual Warfare
Temptations
Things that will close the Windows of Heaven
True Worship and Praise
Understanding God's Principles of Holiness
Understanding God's Way to Financial
Prosperity – Finance Convention '92
Understanding the Seasons of Sowing and Reaping
Unmasking the Devil and His Deceptions
The Weapons of Prayer
Unforgiveness: A Hindrance to Faith
How to Believe with the Heart (Part I)
How to Believe with the Heart (Part II)
Revival

Non-Series Tapes by Pastor Creflo A. Dollar Jr.

Commitment
A Revelation of Love
Commitment
Committing to Serve
Commitment to Love
Commitment to a Greater Covenant
Making a Commitment to the Body of Christ
Committing to the Fear of the Lord
The Hindrances of Commitment (Part 1)
The Hindrances of Commitment (Part 2)
Committing to Jesus Christ (Part 1)
Committing to Jesus Christ (Part 2)
Making a Commitment to Do God's Will
Committing to the Love Covenant

Faith
The God Kind of Faith: Acting on the Word (Part 1)
The God Kind of Faith: Acting on the Word (Part 2)
Faith: The Evidence of the Unseen
Faith: More than Belief
Faith: The Key to the Word
The Difference Between Faith and Belief
Now Faith
The Mind: The Arena of Faith (Part 1)
The Mind: The Arena of Faith (Part 2)
Unforgiveness: A Hindrance to Faith
The God Kind of Faith: What is it?
How Faith Comes (Part 1)
What is Faith?
Faith: The Key to the Spirit Realm
How to Believe With the Heart (Part 1)
How to Believe With the Heart (Part 2)
How to Turn Your Faith Loose
The Principles of Faith

Jesus
The Purpose of Death, Burial and Resurrections

Books by Creflo Dollar

Uprooting the Spirit of Fear	#10UP	$5.99
Understanding God's Purpose for the Anointing	#09001P	$7.95
Capturing the Reality of Heaven and Hell	#002H	$1.99
Confidence: The Missing Substance of Faith	#004C	$1.99
Exposing The Spirit of Competitive Jealousy	#005E	$1.99
The Divine Order of Faith: How to Get from the Problem to the Answer	#006D	$8.95
The Force of Integrity	#008F	$1.99
Rightness vs. Righteousness	#009R	$1.99
Hearing from God and Walking in the Comfort of the Holy Spirit	#BM101	$1.00
Lasciviousness: The Results of Neglect	#BM102	$1.00
Attitudes	#BM103	$1.00
The Sins of The Mouth	#BM104	$1.00
Deliverance From Fear	#BM105	$1.00

BECOME A PARTNER WITH
WORLD CHANGERS MINISTRIES
PARTNERSHIP HAS MEANING!

A partner is...

One who shares responsibility in some common activity with another individual or group.

The vision is...

To teach the Word of God with simplicity and understanding so that it may be applied to our everyday lives in a practical and effective manner. We are being transformed into World Changers – changing our immediate world and all those whom we come in contact with, ultimately making a mark that cannot be erased.

Our part is to...

1. Pray for you on a continual basis.
2. Study and diligently seek the Work of God.
3. Pray that God's blessings be upon you.

Your part is to...

1. Pray for us always.
2. Be committed to support meetings in your area.
3. Support us financially with your monthly pledge.
   "Not because I desire a gift; but I desire fruit that may abound to your account." (Phillipians 4:17)
4. Always uplift the ministry, the Pastor and his family with the words you speak.

To become a partner...

Simply fill out the Vision Partner reply form attached and mail it in the envelope supplied to:

World Changers Ministries Inc.
P.O. Box 490124
College Park, GA 30349
(404) 996 • 0450

May God's richest and best be yours.

I'd like to become a Vision Partner in prayer and financial support with World Changers Ministries Inc.

Last name   First name   Middle initial

Street address   Apartment

City   State   Zip code

You can count on me for a monthly pledge of:

[ ] $500 [ ] $100 [ ] $50 [ ] $10

[ ] Or a one time gift of $_____

I listen to the radio broadcast on:

_____ (Station call letters)

I watch the television broadcast on:

_____ (Station letters / channel)

If you have a prayer request, please include it here:

_____

_____

_____

_____

_____

_____

_____

_____

_____

_____